14.65
397

CHANUTE PUBLIC LIBRARY
111 North Lincoln
CHANUTE, KS 66720

This House Is Haunted!

by
Elizabeth P. Hoffman

A

Book

From
RAINTREE PUBLISHERS
Milwaukee

Copyright © 1977 by Contemporary Perspectives, Inc.

All rights reserved. No part of this book may be reproduced or utilized in any form or by any means, electronic or mechanical, including photocopying, recording, or by any information storage and retrieval system, without permission in writing from the Distributor and Publisher. Inquiries should be addressed to the
DISTRIBUTOR: Raintree Publishers, 310 West Wisconsin Avenue, Milwaukee, Wisconsin 53203 and the PUBLISHER: Contemporary Perspectives, Inc., Suite 6A, 230 East 48th Street, New York, New York 10017.

10 11 12 13 14 15 16 17 18 19   95 94 93 92 91 90

Library of Congress Number: 77-10981

Art and Photo Credits

Cover illustration, Lynn Sweat
Illustrations on pages 8, 14, 18, 21, 34, and 37, Wayne Atkinson.
Photos on pages 12, 13, 20, 25, 26, 30, 38, 43, 44, and 47, courtesy of Elizabeth P. Hoffman.
Every effort has been made to trace the ownership of all copyrighted material in this book and to obtain permission for its use.

Library of Congress Cataloging in Publication Data

Hoffman, Elizabeth, 1921-
   This house is haunted!

   SUMMARY: The author describes the house she and her family moved into, only to discover it was haunted.
   1. Ghosts—Pennsylvania—Beechwood—Juvenile literature. 2. Hoffman, Elizabeth, 1921- —Juvenile literature. 3. Beechwood, Pa.—Biography—Juvenile literature. [Ghosts—Pennsylvania] I. Title.
BF1472.U6H635   133.1'29'74814   77-10981
ISBN 0-8172-1033-4 lib. bdg.

Manufactured in the United States of America.
ISBN 0-8172-1033-4

CHANUTE PUBLIC LIBRARY
111 North Lincoln
CHANUTE, KS 66720

Contents

Chapter 1
  The Dream   5

Chapter 2
  We Find Our House   10

Chapter 3
  Knives and Scissors   16

Chapter 4
  The Lady in the Hall   23

Chapter 5
  Clara!   29

Chapter 6
  Arthur Ford Pays a Visit   36

Chapter 7
  Eileen Garrett Helps Us   41

The Dream

Chapter 1

The author of this story claims that it is a true one. She lives in a house that is a "haunted, but happy, home."

I first saw our home in a dream. The dream seemed so real I almost believed it had happened. I dreamed we were living in a big, old house. There was a large yard with flower beds and a small stream flowing under a *springhouse* (a small storehouse built over water that bubbles from the ground).

Our three sons and our daughter were playing with a frog they had caught near the stream. When I called them for dinner, they began to argue. They wanted to bring the frog with them.

Toward the end of dinner, strange noises began to come from where our youngest son was sitting. Soon we discovered he had hidden the frog under his shirt. His father ordered him to his room. In the dream, I watched him climb two flights of stairs to his room on the third floor. When I awoke from my dream, I was surprised to find myself in my own home. I had no way of knowing it then, but that dream would soon change my life!

At dinner that evening I described the house I had seen in my dream. My family agreed it would be just great to live in my fantastic dream house.

Several weeks later I again dreamed of the same house. This time it was winter. The family was playing with our cats in the living room near the warm fireplace. I saw another fireplace lighting up the room beyond the hall. The next day I told this dream to my children—Robert, Timothy, Wynne, and Pamela—and to my husband, Bill.

Over the next few months, my dreams about this house continued. So did my talks with my family. By this time I was certain that this house was real. I felt it was somewhere nearby, east of where we were presently living. It was hard to believe that a house with such a large backyard could be so close to the city. But there it was in my dreams!

It became a family game to look for *our* house. On Sunday afternoons, we drove through streets in nearby communities, but we couldn't find the right house. We would describe the house to neighbors and friends, never telling them it was from a dream. They just shook their heads and said they didn't know any such place. A house with fireplaces, a springhouse, and a stream, they all agreed, would be farther out in the country.

Two years passed. Because our children were growing, we decided to look for a larger house. But no house we saw seemed as friendly and as inviting as the one in my dreams.

On a rainy Sunday in late April, I was reading the advertisements for houses in the newspaper. Suddenly, I read a very short one. "Beechwood, Pennsylvania. Eight bedrooms,

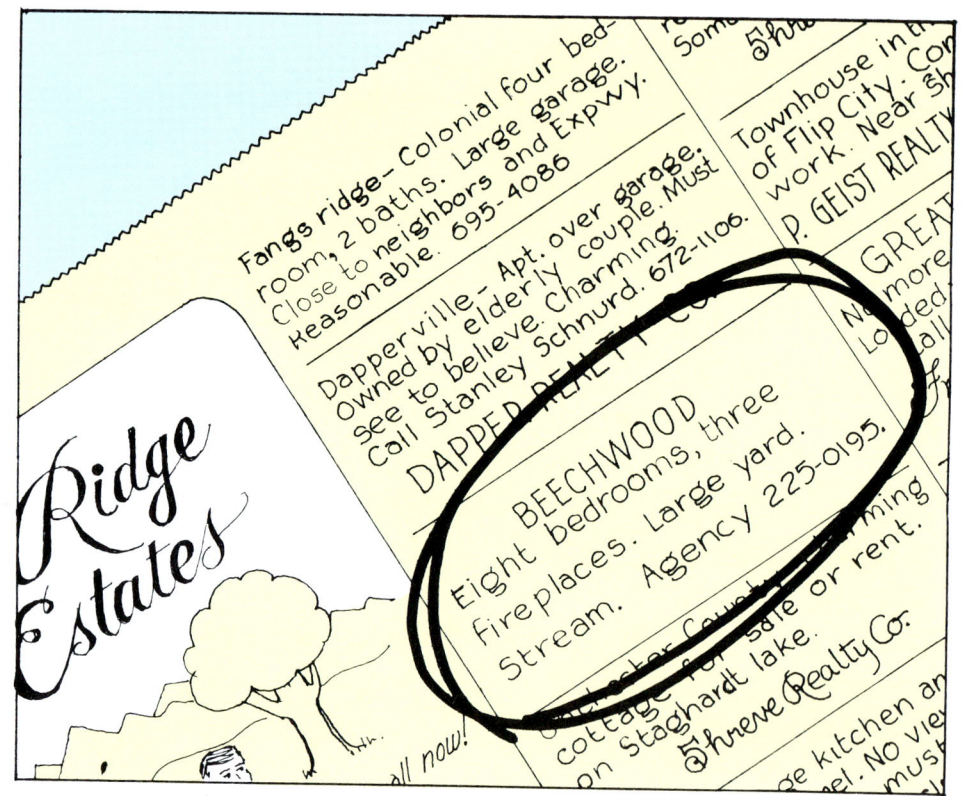

three fireplaces, large yard, stream." I couldn't hold back my excitement. *Could this be our house?*

We had never heard of the town of Beechwood. Was it located many miles out of the city? That would never work. Bill's job was in the central business district, and mine was only two streets from our present house.

But I couldn't get the description of the Beechwood house out of my mind. I dialed the telephone number listed in the ad. A recording told me to call the next day. After waiting all this time, one day longer seemed forever.

We Find Our House

Chapter 2

Monday was cold and rainy—more like early January than late April. Hurrying home from my job, I called the real estate office for information. The agent gave me directions on how to reach the house described in the ad. The Beechwood house was only two miles from our home!

Wynne and Pam went with me. Several blocks from our home, we turned onto a familiar road. We had gone house-hunting on this road before, yet I knew this was the right road to the

Beechwood house. Even when the road seemed to dead-end at a railroad bridge, I drove under the bridge and found another road. I turned sharply to the right, and we crossed a bridge over a swiftly moving creek. On the other side was a steep curving hill. As we rounded the last bend to the right, both Wynne and Pam cried together, "Mommy! There's our house!"

There it was, all right—half-hidden by a tall hedge and hemlock trees. Wynne opened the car door. He scrambled out and disappeared around the hedge. Pam followed but I just sat there, staring. I was amazed at how much it looked like my dream house.

A long porch ran across the front of the house. Two doors and several windows were shaded by the porch roof. Seven windows looked out on the trees from both the second and third stories. White walls made the tall house look even taller.

As I started up the sidewalk to the house, Wynne and Pam raced excitedly around the corner of the porch. "Look!" they shouted. "Here's the frog, just as you said. It was in the springhouse! There's a stream, too! There's a

"There it was all right—half hidden by a tall hedge and hemlock trees."

pond, trees, flowers, and a backyard where we can play ball!"

We walked across the porch and looked through the windows. The house was still furnished, but no one lived there. There were fire-

"I was amazed at how much it looked like my dream house."

places in the rooms on either side of the front hall, *just as I had seen them in my dreams!*

I hurried the children back to the car. I had to get the rest of our family. Within an hour we were all back at our dream house. They were as surprised and delighted as we had been. We all

"With our move to our dream house, an amazing adventure began."

agreed it was like stepping into a different world. *Oh, how right we were!*

People don't usually find their homes in dreams, but we did. A few weeks after we found it, we moved into our dream house. With that move we began an amazing adventure that has never ended.

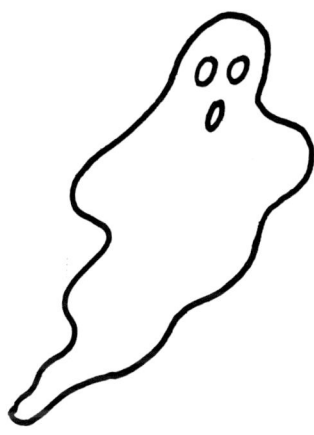

Knives and Scissors

Chapter 3

A few nights after we moved in, I noticed that six-year-old Wynne was sleeping in his bedroom with a pillow over his head. In the morning, I asked him about it.

"Mommy, a lady comes in and looks at me after you turn out the light," Wynne said in a frightened voice.

"Does she do anything? Does she say anything?" I asked, quite sure he was imagining the woman.

"No," he replied. "She just looks at me. I can't sleep with her watching me, so I just put the pillow over my head. Then I can't see her."

I tried to tell him that he was just very tired and that moving into a new room by himself had given him funny ideas. Maybe it was just a shadow or a tree branch outside the window that looked like a woman. Children get funny ideas, and I decided to forget the whole thing.

Then we began to notice some strange things happening. For one thing, the knives in our kitchen seemed to disappear. Every mealtime I had to search everywhere—drawers, the dishwasher, tabletops—to look for a paring knife or the bread knife or the carving knife.

I asked all the boys what they were doing with the knives. They insisted they knew nothing about them. So I continued my search. Bill and I couldn't understand where the knives were going! Our weekly shopping list called for milk, eggs, bread—all the usual items—and *knives*!

We also seemed to be losing our scissors. The sets that belonged with the sewing machine disappeared, one by one, until all four pairs

were gone. The pair we kept in the bathroom was finally located in the basement—broken in two.

By this time, grandmother had come to live with us. She also had trouble holding on to scissors. A large sharp pair hung by a leather strap from the corner of her weaving loom in her room. They vanished during the week the rest of us had gone on a short vacation.

When we returned home, we found grandmother very upset. Her scissors had disappeared when she went to the kitchen to prepare some lunch. She had spent most of Saturday afternoon looking for them. No one could find them. It seemed strange that just the *sharp* knives and the scissors disappeared. The silver table knives we used were never bothered.

We were living in the house almost a year when something odd happened. It made me sure that the children were telling the truth about the missing knives and scissors. Summer vacation had begun. On this particular morning all the children were at the school playground. My housekeeper, Sadie, and I decided to thoroughly clean the dining room. When the front doorbell rang, I put some lining paper and the scissors on the table and went to the door. It was the postman with a package.

When I returned to the dining room, Sadie angrily shouted at me. "Mrs. Hoffman, why did you throw the scissors at me?"

I was shocked. "What did you say?" I asked. She repeated the question. I explained that I certainly had not thrown the scissors at her.

"She pointed to the floor under the table in the middle of the room."

"Well, look for yourself!" She pointed to the floor under the table in the middle of the room. "There they are! I haven't moved away from this door."

Near the center pedestal of the dining room table were the scissors with their points jammed into the carpet. Walking over to them, I leaned down and pulled them out.

"No!" shouted Sadie, "don't come near me with them."

Of course, I had no intention of doing that. I backed over to the buffet and pulled open a drawer. I placed the scissors inside and quickly closed the drawer.

"Sadie," I spoke quietly to the angry woman, "you've worked for me a long time. Surely you know I wouldn't throw scissors at you. I wouldn't harm you in any way. Let's get a cup of coffee and talk about it."

"When you went into the living room," she said, speaking more quietly now, "those scissors *moved across the room*. I really thought you had thrown them."

I explained what I had actually done with the scissors. Then I told her about the problem we were having with knives and scissors.

Sadie was nervous. Her voice trembled. "It's a queer old house," she said. "And I'm not sure I like working here. Sometimes I feel that someone is watching me, but when I look around there's no one there."

Sadie's days with us soon became shorter and further apart, until she told us she didn't want to work for us anymore. "No, the job isn't too hard," she explained, "but the old house just doesn't 'feel' right."

We went through a lot of housekeepers during the next few years.

The Lady in the Hall

Chapter 4

Another grandmother joined our family in Beechwood. My mother now made her home with us. Her room at the end of the second floor hall also opened onto the sun port. It made a small apartment. She usually went to bed around 10 o'clock and rose early.

Mother had been with us about a month when she came down to breakfast one morning, looking very tired. She had a frown on her face as she took her place at the table. Suddenly, she turned to me and angrily asked, "What was the matter with you last night? You kept walking up and down the hall. Your pacing made it impossible for me to sleep. Twice I opened my door to ask you to stop, but each time you disappeared into another room. As soon as I was back in bed and almost asleep, you began again!"

I simply stared at her. I had *not* walked up and down the hall even once during the night. She fussed and fumed. She refused to believe me. For the next few months, my mother complained about my pacing the hall about once a week. When I told her it wasn't me, she insisted it was. "Bill's steps are different," she always said.

Other unusual things happened. One evening Bill was away on a business trip, and the children were all in bed. I was relaxing in our bedroom, reading a new book, when I became aware of a sound coming from the corner near the closet. It sounded as though someone were having trouble breathing . . . like a wheeze or a gasp.

I jumped off the bed and ran to the door, thinking that Tim or Wynne had come for help. But no one was in the hall. The troubled, gaspy

"I ran down the hall to check the bedrooms."

breathing was now behind me in our bedroom. I hurried up the stairs to check on the children. They were all quietly sleeping.

Feeling very uneasy, I sat down on the edge of my bed. Everything was quiet. I thought of things that might make a sound like unhealthy

"I sat down to think of what could have caused the noise."

breathing. Was it the wind blowing through a window crack, or a closet door swinging on a loose hinge, or a rocking chair moving on a floorboard? When Bill returned, I would ask him to look into the problem.

Sometimes friends came by. They would keep their coats on and try to hide their shivering. They often said they were cold in our house. But whenever I looked at the thermometer, it always showed that the room was warm enough. A heating company repairman inspected the rooms and the furnace, but he couldn't do anything about the cold spots.

Then one Saturday morning, my daughter Pam came racing down the stairs. She seemed quite puzzled. "Mom, who was that lady in the hall? She didn't say hello, she just looked at me. And she was wearing a funny dress."

"I don't know," I answered. "Maybe your grandmother has a friend here. Let's go see."

We went up the stairs together. No one was in the hall. We knocked on my mother's door. When she opened it, she was alone. When I asked if she had a visitor, she said, "Of course not. On a Saturday morning?" A hurried search of the other bedrooms revealed no one.

"But Mom, I saw her! She was standing right here looking out the window. Then she turned and looked at me."

I tried to tell her that she had just *thought* she saw someone. Her mind was busy, I told her. A moving shadow from the tree outside had played a trick on her. But Pam was only halfway convinced. *And so was I.*

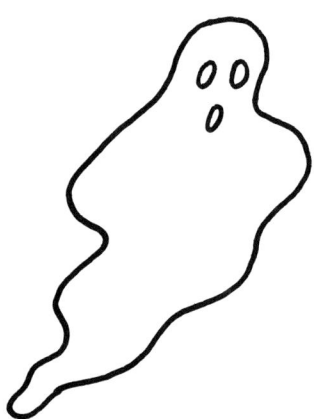

Clara!

Chapter 5

Bill and I knew we had to discuss these strange events. Footsteps when no one was around! Strange sounds heard at night! Knives and scissors missing! A lady in the hall! We had heard of haunted houses, but people like us didn't live in them. We began to keep a record of our unusual events—like cats raising their backs to be petted when we didn't see anyone there. Or a chair that rocked evenly for almost an hour. Or footsteps walking up and down the halls.

We read several books about houses that were haunted. We also searched for and met

"We often heard footsteps."

people who seriously studied hauntings. One of them suggested that when we heard footsteps or suddenly felt cold or heard wheezy breathing, we should call out names to see if there would be any kind of reaction. So we began to do that.

When we saw the rocking chair swaying, we said, "Please stop rocking the chair and go away, John . . . Mary . . . Susan . . . William . . . Sarah . . . Martha . . . Jeffrey. . . ."

"Who was rocking in the chair?"

We repeated as many names as we knew, but nothing happened. If we heard footsteps, we did the same thing. Again nothing happened. Then, one day I was playing the piano when I heard a breathing sound in the music room.

"Go away, Clara," I said. "Please go away." The breathing stopped! I realized we hadn't used the name *Clara* before. Was it *coincidence* that the breathing stopped, or had I found the name of this spirit with troubled breathing?

By now we were convinced that our house had an unseen visitor—a *ghost,* if you like—but we really didn't want to admit it. We had learned that there were many serious, intelligent people who believed in ghosts. As we read their books or listened to them talk, we began to realize that our dream house was *haunted*!

One summer night we went to bed very late. We were leaving the next morning on a trip, and there had been a million things to do. When we finally turned out the light, we were tired and ready to sleep. We noticed a small gleam of light moving back and forth in a straight line just beyond the foot of our bed. This time we both saw it.

"It's probably a *reflection* from a car in the street," Bill said.

I arose and looked out the window. There was no car parked or moving past the house. I listened, but I couldn't even hear one. Our car was parked in the garage with the door closed.

Then I whispered to Bill. "Do you mind if I try something? I have an idea."

He shrugged. "Go ahead."

"Clara," I began, "we are very tired and we have a long day ahead of us. We need to get some sleep. If it really is you, would you please go away so we can rest? We'll try to communicate with you when we come back from our trip. But please, Clara, go away now."

As we watched, the light faded and disappeared. What was it? We still don't know. It was a small dot of light, like a gleam from a pin or ring. It had moved in a straight line for about eight feet. Was a spirit or ghost really there? What did it mean?

When we returned from our trip, I began to research old deeds and other records. I talked

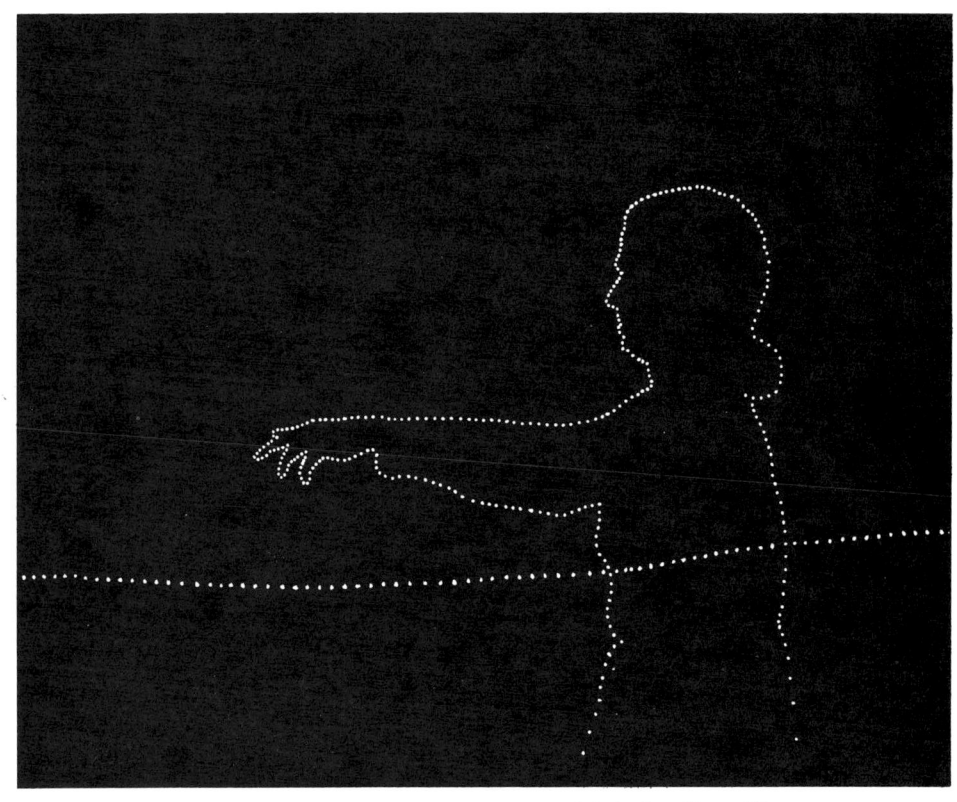
"Could the moving spot of light be Clara?"

with people who had lived in our community. Finally, we learned that a woman named Clarinda Johnson had owned our house. Had Clarinda become a ghost named Clara? It seemed so.

So Clara became an unwanted and unloved part of our family. When the rocking chair moved, we shouted at her to go away. When the laundry fell—three or four times—from the railing in the hall where it had been placed for sorting, we yelled at Clara to leave it alone. When a neighbor told us she saw a strange elderly lady watching her from the window, we knew it was Clara.

Wynne stopped sleeping with his head under the pillow. "I talked to Clara one night," he explained. "She said she wouldn't hurt me."

"Did you really hear her voice?" I asked.

"No, but I knew what she was thinking."

Kids really are strange sometimes.

Arthur Ford Pays a Visit

Chapter 6

One day a friend telephoned us. She said that one of the best *psychics* in America had just agreed to come to Philadelphia to give a lecture. He would also moderate a radio talk show.

[A psychic "feels" or "sees" things without using his fingers or eyes. Sometimes we say he has *ESP*—a special sense unlike the other senses.]

We had joined several clubs and learned more about ghosts, haunted houses, and other unusual subjects. The friend who had called us was the president of one of these clubs. She also asked if I wanted to be a guest on the radio talk show. I could talk with Mr. Arthur Ford about our house and its ghost called Clara.

At last I would have an opportunity to talk with someone who really knew about ghosts. The club president and I planned the evening.

Mr. Ford would give his lecture at eight o'clock. Afterwards, he and a few friends would come to our home to relax and have some refreshments before going to the nearby radio station. We agreed that no one would mention our ghost or anything else about our home. There would be time for that during the show. Mr. Ford would be arriving after dark, so he wouldn't be able to see the yard or anything else outside our house.

As it grew near time to leave for the radio station, Mr. Ford excused himself to freshen up before he left. When he returned to the living

"We all sat in the living room and Arthur Ford told us he had just met 'Clara'."

room several minutes later, he astonished everyone there when he said, "I just met your friend Clara in the upstairs hall. She was standing by the window and she was pointing outside." He then described Clara as we had often seen her. He said she was short. She wore a long, dark dress and had her hair pulled back into a bun. He described her face just as we had seen it.

Then he told us, "She was drowned, you know. Do you have a pond out there? I saw her in my mind being pulled down in the water."

I described the pond in our yard.

"No, no," he protested, "not a pond like that. It was more like a lake. It's where they watered the horses, sheep, and cattle when this house was a farmhouse."

No one had mentioned water or anything about the history of our house. No one but our neighbors, Bill, and I knew about it. I described the old lake that used to be close by.

"Yes," said Mr. Ford, "I saw her drowning there."

On the way to the radio station, I had many questions. Was he sure of what he had seen?

Yes. How did he know her name was Clara? *He had heard it in his mind.* Why did he think our house was once a farmhouse? It didn't look like one. *He saw it in his mind.*

We became friends with Mr. Ford. He visited us several times. Following his directions, we read through old newspapers looking for a report of a drowning. After several months of searching, we found an article telling of the drowning of a woman named Jane Johnson. She had lived in our community. However, it wasn't Clara. It was her cousin.

When we reported this to Mr. Ford, he explained that he had made a mistake. He had seen a woman in the hall pointing out the window. He had received a message from her that her name was Clara. Then he saw the woman in the lake and believed Clara to be the same person. Obviously, it was not Clara. So we still didn't know much more about her.

But in Mr. Ford we did have a new friend and a new teacher. And our haunted house kept making things happen in our lives.

Eileen Garrett Helps Us

Chapter 7

Months passed and Clara continued to haunt us. She didn't appear every day or every week. Sometimes a month or two would go by and nothing would happen. But she made her presence felt. New friends, not knowing anything about our haunted house, would tell us they *felt* something strange there. Meanwhile, we were researching the history of our house. We talked with many people who had information about it.

A local television station presented a show about our house. We were constantly bothered for a month afterwards! People telephoned us to talk to Clara! Or they rang the doorbell and asked if they could walk through our house!

A friend suggested we contact Eileen Garrett in New York and ask her to remove our ghost. Mrs. Garrett was a psychic. Our friend wrote to Mrs. Garrett and told her he had found a house he believed was haunted. He didn't tell her about our family or the story of the house.

We waited a long time for an answer. Finally, a letter arrived from Mrs. Garrett. She would visit our home *if* we agreed to her terms. First, no children were to be present. Second, we were not to talk with her until she indicated she was ready. And third, she wanted permission to record our conversations and to take photographs for her psychic organization. We agreed and set a date for Mrs. Garrett's visit.

When the doorbell rang on that special Tuesday, Bill and I answered it together. Mrs. Garrett and her secretary entered. They were followed by a photographer, a man with a tape recorder, a man with floodlights, and two observers. They all scattered through the rooms on the first floor, while Mrs. Garrett sat down in a chair near the bookcase. For some time, she

"Eileen Garrett, her secretary, and her staff were at the door."

"The music room always seemed to be cold no matter what we did."

studied the room carefully and stared at us. Finally, she began to speak.

She told us we had been led to this house for a reason—to have experiences that would help us to grow and learn. (I thought back to my many dreams of the house.) Then she told us about our children. She said Clara liked them, although Clara really didn't like children. No one had told Mrs. Garrett what kind of haunting we had. No one had told her the ghost's name. How did she know? She sensed my question.

"Your Clara is here," she said. "I see her and feel her. I will speak for her." Then Mrs. Garrett walked to the music room and sat down in the rocking chair. But why in the rocking chair? There were four other chairs and a sofa she could have chosen. She closed her eyes and began to speak. She lost her own Irish accent and began to speak with a New England accent.

Mrs. Garrett said Clara was speaking through her. Clara had come to our house from Vermont. She was a widow with one son and a niece. Another son had died when he was a little boy. She used the farm to breed, raise, and trade horses. She vowed she would become the best horse trader in the state. This made her very unpopular, as women were not supposed to do such work. But Clara thought for herself, took care of herself, and supported her family.

People did not like her so she did not make friends. Her only son was killed in an accident.

This left her lonely and very unhappy. She lived in the house with her niece. She grew to hate people and believed they hated her. Although she wanted to be loved, she did nothing to encourage people to love her.

Clara accidentally fell down the narrow stairs to the cellar one day and badly injured her head. She was afraid a doctor might need to operate on her and cut her head, so she hid all the knives and scissors in the house. Her head injury grew worse because she didn't get help. An infection finally caused her death. But her spirit, being very confused and still needing love, didn't leave the house. It still looked for knives and scissors. Or it paced up and down the hall as she had done when she was alive and in pain.

Finally, I asked Mrs. Garrett if she would send Clara away. She refused, saying that was *our* task. She would, however, tell us how to do it. With a few friends, we were to sit in the music room several times a week and pray for Clara's rest. We were to say aloud that we loved her and wished her well. We were to think of her with kindness, and we were to tell her that she must leave this house to go to her new life.

"Were we finally rid of 'Clara'?"

This task was difficult, but we decided to try. Two or three times a week, for several months, we did what Mrs. Garrett had directed. Gradually, the sound of footsteps disappeared. The rocking chair didn't move except when a real person sat in it. The cold damp spots also disappeared.

We thought that after Clara left our house, it would be the end of our hauntings. It wasn't! The other "inmates of our inn," as we call them, are not nearly as bothersome as Clara had been.

Occasionally, we smell the smoke from the pipe of a one-legged sailor who stomps through the hall. Or we hear a young girl crying. Several psychic friends have been working to identify *these* trapped spirits.

Sometimes, now that the children are grown and married, we think we should find a smaller house. But we really don't want to leave. Instead, we have built a swimming pool. During the digging we have uncovered dishes, farm tools, and bits of old glass. We even found part of an old clay pipe! We have our own historical finds, and we're still learning more about our house.

Our house is now haunted by happy memories. And who knows, in the next hundred years more ghosts may turn up! Maybe they'll be our own ghosts!